AF270606

Ancient Civilizations

DiscoverRoo
An Imprint of Pop!
popbooksonline.com

THE AZTECS

by Elizabeth Andrews

WELCOME TO DiscoverRoo!

This book is filled with videos, puzzles, games, and more! Scan the QR codes* while you read, or visit the website below to make this book pop.

popbooksonline.com/aztecs

abdobooks.com

Published by Pop!, a division of ABDO, PO Box 398166, Minneapolis, Minnesota 55439. Copyright © 2023 by Abdo Consulting Group, Inc. International copyrights reserved in all countries. No part of this book may be reproduced in any form without written permission from the publisher. DiscoverRoo™ is a trademark and logo of Pop!.

Printed in the United States of America, North Mankato, Minnesota.
102022
012023

THIS BOOK CONTAINS RECYCLED MATERIALS

Cover Photo: DE AGOSTINI PICTURE LIBRARY/Getty Images, Shutterstock Images
Interior Photos: Wikimedia Commons, Historia/Shutterstock, Glasshouse Images/Shutterstock, Dorling Kindersley/Getty Images, North Wind Picture Archives/Alamy Stock Photo, Nastasic/Getty Images
Editor: Emily Dreher
Series Designer: Laura Graphenteen

Library of Congress Control Number: 2022941102

Publisher's Cataloging-in-Publication Data

Names: Andrews, Elizabeth, author.
Title: The Aztecs / by Elizabeth Andrews
Description: Minneapolis, Minnesota : Pop!, 2023 | Series: Ancient civilizations | Includes online resources and index.
Identifiers: ISBN 9781098243272 (lib. bdg.) | ISBN 9781098243975 (ebook)
Subjects: LCSH: Mexico--History--Juvenile literature. | Aztec Indians--Juvenile literature. | Ancient civilization--Juvenile literature. | Indigenous peoples--Social life and customs--Juvenile literature. | Cultural anthropology--Juvenile literature.
Classification: DDC 972.01--dc23

*Scanning QR codes requires a web-enabled smart device with a QR code reader app and a camera.

CONTENTS

The Aztec people began as a wandering clan called the Mexicas in the 1200s. Their homeland is a mystery, but they may have traveled from northern Mexico. A **priest** had a vision that the community

Tenochtitlán was well organized. It had palaces, temples, roads, canals, and small houses.

should next settle on an island in Lake

Texcoco. That island became the city

of Tenochtitlán.

The Aztecs who lived on Tenochtitlán were controlled by a city called Atzcapotzalco. They had to fight in its military and pay tributes. In 1426 a dangerous ruler came into power.

The alliance of Tenochtitlán, Texcoco, and Tlacopan was called the Aztec Triple Alliance.

The Aztecs didn't want to support the city any longer.

The Aztec leader Itzcóatl gathered help from neighbors. They fought a 114-day war against Atzcapotzalco and won. An alliance in the Valley of Mexico between the people of Tenochtitlán, Texcoco, and Tlacopan officially started the Aztec empire. Tenochtitlán was the capital city.

The Aztecs needed resources and wealth to be a successful empire. They **invaded** towns near Lake Texcoco and farther into the mountains and valley around them. The **conquered** towns became **city-states** of the Aztec Empire. They paid tributes to the empire.

Tributes were goods and services, like cloth, food, animal skins, and **ceremonial** costumes.

In 1440, an emperor named Montezuma I spread the empire past the Valley of Mexico, all the way to the Gulf of

Mexico. The empire continued expanding and collecting more city-states until 1502.

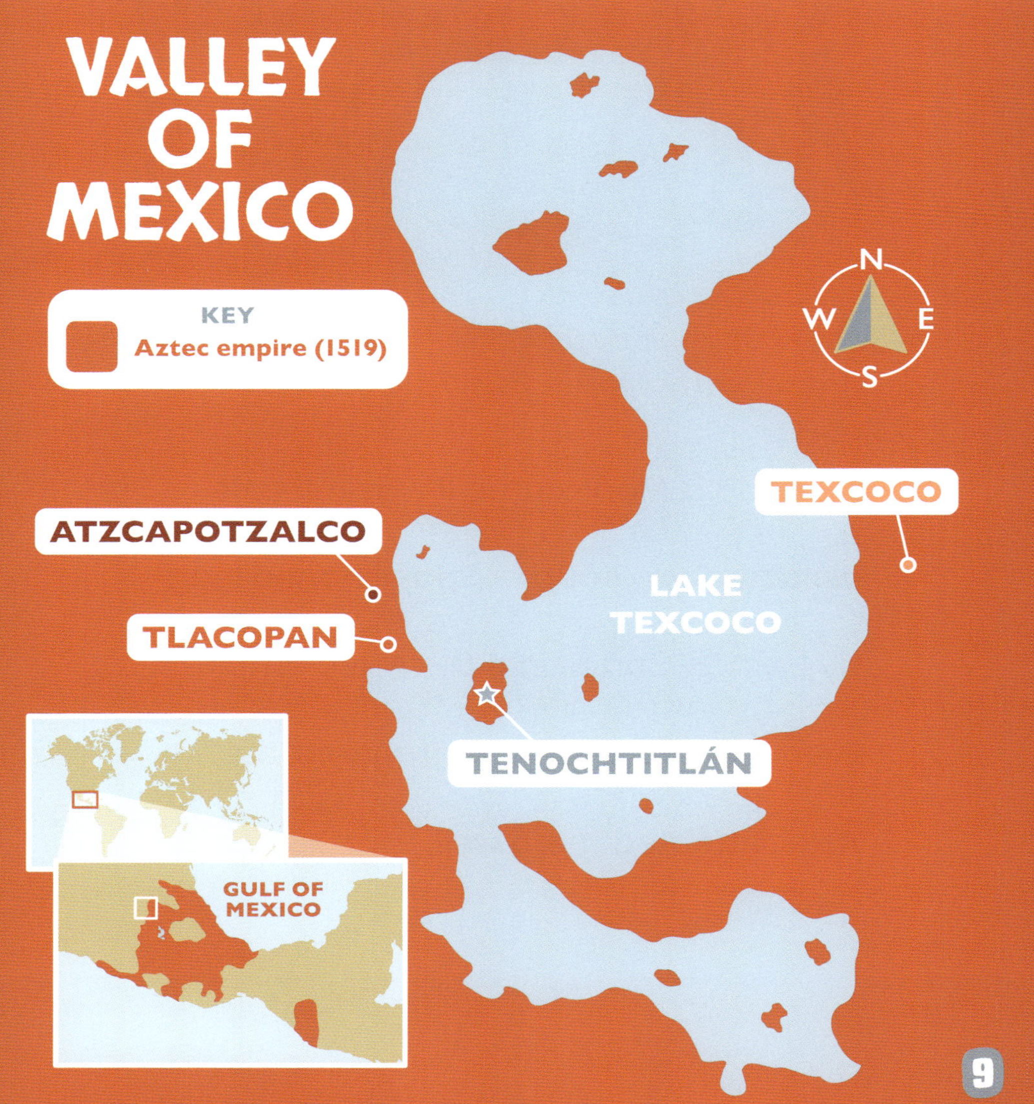

The Spanish army fought with weapons the Aztecs had never seen before.

In 1519, Montezuma II was ruler. He welcomed a group of Spanish men lead by Hernán Cortés into the Aztec empire. Even though they were strangers, the Aztecs treated them well.

But the Spanish attacked the Aztecs. For two years, Aztec warriors defended their home, but the Spanish were too powerful. They also carried **smallpox** with them. The disease killed 40 percent of the Aztec people in one year. It weakened the Aztecs to the Spanish invasion. In 1521, Tenochtitlán was officially captured. The Aztec empire fell.

POSITIONS OF POWER

The Aztec empire started as three main **city-states** around Lake Texcoco.

Eventually, more tribes were **conquered** and they joined the empire. All power in the Aztec empire was held by an emperor

from Tenochtitlán. Emperors were

considered godlike. They were respected

and feared.

Each city-state had official leaders who served the emperor. They oversaw the military, temples, and laws, and owned all state land. A council of chosen men related to the emperor helped run smaller sections of the city-states. They collected tributes, served as judges and military leaders, and organized education. All public officials were **nobility**.

Warriors were very important to ancient Aztecs. They fought for new land and resources to bring wealth to the

empire. Being a warrior was
sacred. This meant
the fighting was
done to please
the gods. Every
new emperor first
had to prove themself
worthy by winning new
lands. Commoners
and nobility could
be warriors.

Aztec headdresses were made from the feathers of the quetzal bird.

Aztec enemies feared meeting jaguar and eagle warriors on the battlefield.

As a warrior spent more time in the Aztec military, he would rise in rank. This would also change his position in Aztec society. Even if the warrior was a commoner, he could become as powerful and respected as a noble. Two of the highest ranks were the jaguar and eagle. To reach these ranks, the warrior had to capture four enemies and perform many acts of bravery.

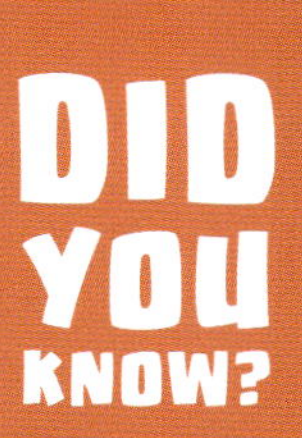

DID YOU KNOW?

Warriors wore battle costumes that matched their ranks. Eagle warriors wore eagle-shaped headdresses and suits made of feathers.

LIFE IN THE EMPIRE

Social status played a big role in the daily life of an Aztec. It determined a person's jobs, clothes, home, and marriages. Men and women were treated as equals, though their daily work differed. Men were the leaders of the family and worked

outside the home. Women worked in the home. Their most important task was raising the children. The children's education began when they turned eight.

Aztecs used canoes to move around the lake and canals. They were made from logs hollowed out by fire.

Nobles married other nobles to form alliances between **city-states**. They lived in big homes with servants. Nobles ate meat, fish, and chocolate. They wore cotton clothes and jewelry. Showing off their wealth was important. Emperors wanted the differences between nobility and commoners to be clear.

Commoners were tradesmen, farmers, and craftsman. Some farmed community land. The land needed to be farmed continually or it would be

DID YOU KNOW?

All boys were trained to be warriors. It was a great honor to protect the empire.

taken back by government officials.

Commoners had to give part of the crops farmed to the empire as tribute. They wore rougher clothing and ate mostly grains, fruits, and vegetables.

The island city of Tenochtitlán was the center of Aztec life. It was home to more than 140,000 people. Aztecs were very advanced at city planning. The royal palaces and temples were on the island. There were good, straight roads and well-designed **canals** that made travel in and out of the city easy. Marketplaces were set up on the island and along Lake Texcoco's shores.

Craftsmen created statues, feathered cloaks and headdresses, costumes, and masks decorated with precious stones. Aztecs built furniture and boats. The goods were sold at marketplaces around the empire.

The Aztec played a ball game called *ollama*. The goal of the game was to get a rubber ball through a stone hoop. Players couldn't use their hands. They had to use their hips, head, elbows, and knees. The game often turned violent.

CHAPTER 4

FOR THE GODS

The Aztec empire followed a polytheistic religion. They worshipped many gods. When new land was **conquered**, Aztecs brought the gods and goddesses of those places into their own religion. Nearly all aspects of Aztec life revolved around honoring the gods.

Temples were designed to look like mountains rising high above Aztec cities.

Rituals and **ceremonies** were held to mark the passing of seasons, to honor a new emperor or good harvest, and to ask the gods for help. Members of all social classes participated in the feasts, dances, and celebrations that occurred during ceremonies.

An important god to the Aztecs was Huitzilopochtli. He was the god of the sun and war, born from the earth goddess. The Aztecs believed he needed an offering of human blood every day. So, they would **sacrifice** people for Huitzilopochtli. Human sacrifice was a common practice with the Aztecs. People considered it an

DID YOU KNOW?

Warriors who died in battle were said to return to earth as hummingbirds. Huitzilopochtli was said to appear as a hummingbird.

honor to be offered to the gods. Most

sacrificed people were prisoners and

captives from war.

Temples hosted ceremonies. The temples were beautiful examples of the Aztec's building and decorating skills. Templo Mayor stood at the center

The Templo Mayor was the heart of the Aztec empire.

of Tenochtitlán. Atop it was a pyramid dedicated to Huitzilopochtli and Tlaloc, the god of rain. It was decorated with staircases and snake heads. Parts of Templo Mayor are still being discovered today!

The Aztec Empire may have fallen, but it still influences the modern world. Its mark can be seen in the Nahua people of Mexico. They are living descendants of the Aztecs. Aztec religion has inspired modern artists. And the capital of Mexico was built from the ruins of Tenochtitlán.

MAKING CONNECTIONS

TEXT-TO-SELF

If you lived in the Aztec empire, would you have wanted your home to be on the island of Tenochtitlán or off it? Please explain.

TEXT-TO-TEXT

Have you read any other books about ancient civilizations that existed in Mexico? If so, what did they have in common with the Aztecs?

TEXT-TO-WORLD

What do you think would have happened to the Aztecs if the Spanish never arrived? How would Mexico be different?

GLOSSARY

canal — a channel of water made by humans for boat transportation or for bringing water to crops.

ceremony — a formal event or ritual held on a special occasion.

city-state — a state made of a city and its surrounding territory.

conquer — to gain land by force.

invade — to enter an area by force, in order to conquer.

noble — a person of high rank or title.

priest — a person who oversees ceremonies, prayers, and offerings to the gods.

sacrifice — a person or animal killed as an offering to please a god.

smallpox — a sickness that causes fever, skin marks, and often death.

INDEX

popbooksonline.com/aztecs

*Scanning QR codes requires a web-enabled smart device with a QR code reader app and a camera.